Tenuous Chapel

ABZ Series in Poetry

Tenuous Chapel

poems by

Melissa Tuckey

ABZ

ABZ POETRY PRESS

All inquiries and permission requests should be
addressed to the Editor, ABZ Press, PO Box 2746,
Huntington WV 25727-2746.

CATALOGING DATA
Tuckey, Melissa
  Tenuous chapel / Melissa Tuckey.   1st ed.
    p.   cm.   (ABZ First Book Poetry Series)
  ISBN-13: 978-0-9801560-5-8 (pbk.   alk. paper)

Library of Congress Control Number: 2012950064

I. Title. II. Series

CONTENTS

III. WHEN THE GIRAFFES COME

FOREWORD

Many years ago, working one summer in a big bookstore on Fifth Avenue in New York City, I spent long, tedious hours watching customers browsing among books, turning their pages and reading a bit, or looking at pictures, and eventually noticed that the most interesting people to watch were the ones in the poetry section, especially those who appeared to have stumbled there by accident. Most likely killing time while waiting for someone, they would pull a small, thin volume off the shelf, open it at random, glance at a poem and put it right back on the shelf. Sometimes, though, they would hesitate, continue reading, turn to another poem and read that one thoughtfully, then check the name of the author, the price of the book, and read some more poems before proceeding to the cash register. This is a seduction scene, I thought to myself. Terse, startling and instantly captivating, this is how poetry casts its spell and makes people lose their heads.

When I first read *Tenuous Chapel* by Melissa Tuckey that's what happened to me. Of course, in her case I had no idea who the author was. The manuscript came to me in the mail with a bunch of others, all without a name or any information about the poets. The poems were short, often cryptic and yet striking. If the hope of any poem is to render experience in a fresh, unsettling way, she has that gift. She likes to disorient us, pull the rug from under our expectations, and to do so quickly and decisively, so we catch our breath in astonishment and delight. Here, for instance, is the first poem in her book.

O, Piano

After John Cage

I've lassoed the enormous weight of you
shipped you across the continent
carried you up three flights of stairs

but still I do not know
what you eat

Such leaps of the imagination in poetry are exhilarating.
They make even a short poem like this one seem a miracle.
We read it again and again to re-experience the jolt of its
ending and penetrate its meaning. In a poem called "Re:
Acquittal of Generals," she has a snowman sunbathing
duct-taped to a lawn chair juxtaposed to some generals
arguing that they aren't in control of their men. This
happens again and again in her book. Beauty and terror
collide, or they exist side by side. A dark shadow of war
falls over the lives of people in her poems. Nothing is
spelled out, but there's an unmistakable feel of despair
and catastrophe in the air, of what she calls "the emptiness
that becomes/a nation on the eve of its own casualty." In
one poem she has the German philosopher Hegel claim
that we ought not to worry about separating the darks from
lights at the end of history, since everything will turn out
pink, but that, clearly, is not her view. A soldier, in another
one of her poems, asks:

How can I demolish
the house of my enemy

the house is my own suffering
and inside the children
of my suffering multiply.

Tuckey is a lyric poet of the type that believes everything can be said in a few words. Even when she recalls her family and her childhood experiences, her intent is always to be concise, to focus on an image or two and depend on hints to get her meaning across. "It's necessary to be quiet in the hands of the marvelous," A.R.Ammons once said in a poem. Tuckey, too, believes that. She likes the moments when time appears to stands still and one becomes conscious of the light. "Promiscuous light," she calls it, the one that "goes out each day / farther from whatever we've anchored / whatever we can't give away." What she mulls over in her poems, in other words, are remembered things that haunt her life and that she still can't get out of her mind. Not just grandmother's house with a kettle boiling over or her father under an umbrella cooking burgers on a grill, but hearing a cricket chirp once in a closet of an empty house or mistaking the sun going down in the rearview mirror for an ambulance. How beautiful, I kept saying to myself again and again reading her poems. Tuckey may call the chapel in the title of her book "tenuous," but there's nothing flimsy and insubstantial about all the fine poems she has collected here.

Charles Simic

"Split by a tendril of revolt stone cedes to
blossom everywhere"

—Muriel Rukeyser

O, Piano

After John Cage

I've lassoed the enormous weight of you
shipped you across the continent
carried you up three flights of stairs

but still I do not know
what you eat

I. TESTIMONY OF DAYLIGHT

Demeter Falls in Love with Winter

I loved the blinding snow, the whiting out
of all my work, the way the animals stumbled—
the hunger it brought, the need for flesh

My most creative period, nothing
was wasted, everything green
exhausted, the soil fed by bones and blood

O, how the trees moaned and ached, such
sorrow, what did they know of separation?
They lived in groves and wanted nothing more

Fat bears who all summer fed on grapes—
slumbered like babes While the crow
in her murder, dined on dark feasts

I loved the ice, how it encircled
the living and laid flat a bed for my slumber
How it held memory of fire

How stark the light grew, how severe

Empty House

Because the weight of grandmother's death
Three tables inherited from various aunts

Because twelve deer grazing in a winter field
Clothing worn once then tossed

Because shelter, because sleep

Child on the floor with a bowl of plums

We loved the lack of closets

The way paint on the walls could fill a room

Daughter

I am not your soldier. I will not hold
the gun while you puke, will not cradle
the folded flag. This flask
of fire is my own. I will not pour a drink
down your grassy throat.

in wet black
boughs of trees
in the scarred stumps
of wood

These are the flowers I've gathered.
Forsythia buds held tightly
through winter. Roses bent at the neck
bowing in prayer, veins shot.

a foot or a fist
skin the color of sod
bluing green

I am not your lady, not the misses,
nor princess of all things possible.
I am not your favorite little artist.
My name is not a letter home.

a child's broken hand
the bruised rain's
foreign currency

The highway is a sheet of glass
If I hit the brake
with enough force
I can write your name on the guardrail.

God and Country

The wife curls her afternoon body in question
beside the dreaming cats
says I'll have what the sky is having—
golden wisteria, oak rattle, hush of pine

So quickly the sky purples
and horizon casts
its pale light on what remains: the wife exists
to cast her gaze on what fades,
that old country—

country of debt and famine
The one she loves slumped over
his small enterprise, as the light
narrows and sinks

Difficult Music

We sleep with intention
We close our eyes and what enters the dark
place that is the body begins repair

Like paper from lint we carry in pockets
we open cautiously one to the other
accordion of dust on the air

The violins of sleep play through us
We tunnel through houses open doors
looking for whatever it is we lost in daylight

River's flashing current
Body's bright mill turning grain to dust

Aubade

I still don't know the difference
between love and apparition

A horned owl staring from the tree
as if the tree had eyes

Come morning I'll watch your long hair
brush the floor as you tie your shoes

I fill a thermos and pack a lunch I stay
in bed and watch sunlight fill an empty house

How lightly it touches the chair
where you tied your shoes

Baby Grand

Song cut like roses for a still-water vase
thorns bringing blood to the surface

Remember the pleated skirt
the patent leather shoes

the mural above the piano
with its sickness of plaster

The burden of grandfather's skin
its story of bruises

in his hands whatever fat the land gave up
a tomato or an orange

He played the piano
Angels fell from the eaves

Old Soldier's Home

October sage, blue flowers hold summer
heat as memory

Inside the gated cemetery where bronze
faces weather gloom

The bees half drink, half sleep
My friend pets one, it doesn't move

Is it ecstasy that sedates, or panic?

Praise

It was the lightest sort of rain
one could drown in it
without knowing

In the mountains an ark
skeleton of whale

Late night you can hear him on the radio
saying follow me or drown
I listen when I am out of coffee

I remember you filed
your nails with a file
that said "kiss me"

We called that rain *lady rain*
envied the leaves their shining

Ghost Fishing Louisiana

"These people are in prison and there's poison loose."
—Rev. Willie T. Snead Sr., Mossville, LA

That's not an ambulance
that's the sun
going down in your rearview mirror

It gets in your clothes it gets in
the way you talk

And the thunder late at night
railroad cars full of poison
bumping into one another

Gambling boats ghost fishing
on Lake Charles

Sugar is refined here for sweet tea
flour bleached white
men selling melons the size of heads

Her house held the cancer
like fish in a locked box

Doing Hegel's Laundry

He said not to worry about separating
the darks from lights at the end of history
everything would be pink but still

I worried about the ones that said hand wash only
and what about the delicates
lingerie that so heightened his imagination

he spent hours gazing into the lace
did he really want me to throw it all together?
The end of history will come but not

the end of laundry Saturday morning
and the clouds fold above the snap
of one-two, one-two

Evening Tide

The ransacked yard, apple blossoms
chewed to the quick, life taken

A singing bowl
the hills filled with light

The way his hands crescendo
The weight of the keys, each note

Trembling in violet light
Throat to multi-colored throat

Promiscuous light, the subtle blues
of that slow deep rhythm

Evening tide, the way the light goes out each day
farther from whatever we've anchored

whatever we can't give away.

Einstein's Hands

It wasn't the lines on his face the way they question
the light not the raised brow or shock
of white hair
not the subdued grace connecting everything
to everything—

It was his hands carried the burden

Tenuous Chapel

Because we could and no one stopped us
we rode to the top of the glittering world
bright and awake in that hotel lobby
at 4 a.m. to see what it looked like

and you said we could live like this
following one vague notion to the next
to see where we ended up
and for years we did

II. ROPE AS WITNESS

"The fever of metal is the song of this dawn."

—Mahmoud Darwish

Time's Arrow

No one will remember the arsonist
smoking a cigarette
and laughing

The child will remember
letters of the alphabet
rising from flames

windows exploding, fire, a whistle
but who will listen
to ash?

How does history survive?
the language of God in translation

inside every mirrored locket
a portrait of the ocean

Full Snow Moon

The bombers fly so close you feel their engines in your chest
though none can say where they're headed or why

On the lake near my house, boys dare each other
onto the frozen surface

The smallest brings the weight of his fear
He drags it like a shadow

Silent Night

Deep in sleep, we heard the call, abstract at first, and then a ceaseless bickering. In between day and night, in those national years of disaster, we strained to hear instructions but could not make out a single word.

Around the corner came a fire truck, its wide lights sweeping the black street. We clutched our hearts and looked for flames. It was then we saw a fat man dressed in red waving from the truck, at his side a white haired woman tossed candy to the empty street. On the speakers a scratchy rendition of "Silent Night."

Dying Grass Moon

A great aunt, her eyes sinking, a hospital bed
Uncle asleep in front of the television
where we all die   I want to open a window

I've come to be fond of air, to believe in the lungs
that they do what they do without thinking

The blue hills in sunlight what mother saw
as destitute, some rocks we made into pantheon
cedar trees the wind blew down

With every breath
the world disappears more completely

Refrain

A cricket in the closet is the closest
I've come to home, I leave
the windows open nothing comes inside

Late night birds carry the weight
of war I wake with
alarm instead of love

I tell you now I admit it I'm
jealous horses die and you bury
them you know their names

Here on my street people disappear
without ceremony

Rope as Witness

Self as the tongue
of the bell
in churches
and at bedsides
ringing

a tree
bending body
to drink:

drink, self, drink

bell as body
and as rope

from the dark throat
springing:
a bitter
cup of being

Both Flower and Fruit

The kettle whistles for children buried
in a Chinese schoolhouse   A friend looking for tea
opens the drawer, becomes overwhelmed

As if his conscience belonged to someone else
the poet says "I'm not an activist," shrugs a little,
pours his tea,"I can't write about those kind of things"

The correspondent, overwhelmed, weeping,
she was there when they carried the bodies out
The crowd raging and she a foreign object

I find myself weeping because we have the same name
something as trivial as that
puts me inside her voice unable to speak

Yesterday birds with their throats open
not making a sound, the heat
had absolved them of singing

My friends from India say this heat is nothing
We cut open a mango, let it spill on our hands

Both flower and fruit bloom on the air
whatever we call essence, it's only a trace

Elegy for Disappointment

In Moscow a man with a rocket launcher
circles the embassy, art deco fixtures
everything polished and waiting

An old man at the public meeting shakes
his book of poems at us, admonishes
us for knowing nothing!

At midnight our train lurches to a halt
Women shine flashlights on chandeliers
they've come to sell in the snow

Dinner with army contractors
and a woman singing
"summertime and the living is easy"

The sky's a bloodshot eye above
this scar of landscape, smokestacks
in the distance like inch high soldiers

Shot glasses on a darkening bar

Young Valley Farmers

We pass each other from time to time, alarmed
the smiling pig, the boy with his bucket
the happy goose, they follow me
from room to room, singing

Mother tickles the pig with her delicate hands
photographs him in the bathtub
Father carries the sheep to the dining room table
or is it a dog

At night I hear them praying, but it is never night
a yellow sky tricks the day into starting over

We Get Down on Our Knees

The alarm and the planes
Rain clouds on the horizon where silence
moves like a cold front

Loud speakers and a service in Spanish
Watering flowers I get full inside

The car alarm begins again
Our yard is full of lead we can't grow food there

Christ in tulips this year
knotted bulbs
pushing through all that dirt to rise

Portrait of Palestine

Someone's erased her jawbone again
better she have no jaw at all
than a prominent chin

They say the sea's too restless
the horizon too full of promise

They've given her a drab background
and pocket of crushed cigarettes, taken
her veranda—replaced
the valley with a prison courtyard

Laughter used to rise from her mouth like birds
Fish leapt at the sound of her voice

Now they paint her mouth closed
They can't stand
the way she looks at them

Late sunlight/ olive grove/ grave of her mother

Curators worry the mask is cracking

Beneath it all kinds of things we wouldn't want to know

She shouldn't

have left / the house / for water

He shouldn't

have gone / to school / that day

They shouldn't

let their children play / in front of the Mosque

She gave birth crying for water

Who threw the rock? Why'd she mouth off?

Did somebody/   in front of my gun?
              /move/

❧

She wears no jewels

Monument

Waterfalls flank the freedom wall
eagles carry a wreath, or
are they ripping it to shreds?

The pavilion blares its trumpets
and we absorb the emptiness that becomes
a nation on the eve of its own casualty

I want to build a monument
to the guy who drove his tractor
into the fountain

Chapel of Stone

Hands gentled by spirit, bed robed
by concrete, this eternal life
and what the eyes hold

How the light plays you in color
as the sun moves east to west, to round
the blood like that, to bring

Petals of light and how she falls
is falling, never reaches, my God
arms squared to offer balance

Ladies in hats fan themselves
before the heart's great flame
Men gentle like horses

And how moonlike, the ones
who love like bookends
Two hearts in a block of stone

Re: Acquittal of Generals

A snowman
duct-taped to a lawn chair
sunbathing

and the generals

argue
they aren't in control
of their men

Rock Creek Park Runner

The police ask if she is being chased

Yes, I am being chased, she says
if I fall asleep
I will be penetrated by great sadness

The Wheel

Animal therapists build
a treadmill for the elephant because
all he does is lie around

Even the bulbs this spring
bloom out of turn, each waiting
for the other to open

One exasperated soldier:
How can I demolish
the house of my enemy

the house is my own suffering
and inside the children
of my suffering multiply

Snow Globe

National Archives

The snow blows for days and never accumulates

Birds at the feeder too fat to fly

III. WHEN THE GIRAFFES COME

Return

Nothing tangible remains
Yet you can still see the two mirrors
you stood between as a girl
trying to glimpse eternity
Grandmother's face creams and potions
her books about health and Jesus
Grandpa's work boots on the basement stairway
Cigarette smoke hanging at three feet
Smell of all day coffee, pastries and sugars
grandma shouldn't eat
Kids tramping the wooden stairs, the circle
between rooms
Purple violets in the eastern window
His eyes always full after she passed
And what is left? A house with indoor plumbing
A chart on the wall for grandpa's weight
A man like that is disappearing from this world
The rooms too are disappearing
You might have entered were it not for
the world, waking

Portrait of My Father

Rain coming down sideways
umbrella overhead, charcoal fizzing
as he tries to light the flame
to cook our burgers

We huddle in a pop-up trailer bored with our luck
A caricature of himself scotch-taped
to the fridge for decades:
man and his family on vacation

Rain penned him in—
he sketched the hours and the days
artist turned father
turned salesman

He made a choice, mom says
I don't remember the choice, remember only
the gesture—
rain painting my father, a man

Needle

Grandma says I'll go blind
in this light
If I step on a needle
it will go to my heart, I needle-
point *Jesus Loves You*
on a tea towel
in the dim light of rain

This is before stamp collections
before macramé and painting by numbers

She teaches me to cross-
stitch, says *your mother*
will have a heart attack &
can't you stay in for one day—

The bruise on my knee is yellow
I can't stay in for one day

Laura waits outside on her bike
We already know we are witches

History of Small Spaces

Hydrangea you say when
you are looking for reasons
to believe in the soul

Milkweed when you remember
his breath on your neck

The silence of plums
calligraphy of potato vines

chipping paint
of you are home now walls
stained with not now

After awhile you quit asking
where fruit flies come from

The Last Time We Took a Family Vacation

The other night when my drunk aunt
flashed her tits at the whole family

we were horrified and when her daughter
yelled *you're stupid mom* it broke our hearts

but tonight at the bar across from our condo
we find ourselves clapping along

The bar is full of sober people on vacation
lonely in their new clothes

and no one can take their eyes off aunt Rosie
in her beach shorts and bowling shirt

rocking back and forth clapping her hands
yelling *oh yeah oh yeah oh yeah*

Venus and the Space Station

My friend George thinks of spring
in terms of the likelihood of rain
whereas I wander loosely
tree pollen dangling from my hair

When he tills he thinks of children and early peas
On the phone 300 miles away
he tells me I'm confusing
venus with the space station

Says when he dies he wants us to
slap a rocket on his back
send him out to space

I picture him stuck on the neighbor's roof
& us below ringing the bell
asking to borrow a ladder

Anemone

If we touch, hand to wrist, the back of knees
do we forget our names?

I'm willing to risk the horses of delight
to let tributaries of rain course

the lowest point between where
sentiment is breached

even if we can't return

can never find our way back to the surface
to stay here: a punctuated life

where the living grieve
and the dead are always hungry

I'm willing to break with you to burst
into flame or flower

Provincetown

A real gully washer   ratcheted waters

in flood high knickers   my sailor

my white horse   O billow of rain   hellcat run riot

my bull at the gate

my isthmus   wailing wind and whistle

my surge   my Romeo

knock of trestle and track

my windswept home   my promontory   my delirious

sin swept   enraptured tongue of sand

moored and unmooring

monument to the lost and wrecked

Dogwood Winter

Trees run with us
When we stop, they stop

But sometimes in the fog
they keep going

Al Fresco

An unseasonably warm day, the house held its humor.
We worked slowly, covered the peas and lettuce.
Kept indoors until the sun rolled out its reds, made gold
and round everything once flat. We dined on a patio
overlooking the pond where neighbors poked for toads.
Does laughter release joy? They chant and orgy, those
toads.

Walking twilight, we're drawn to the pitch of peepers,
engage in a standoff with a leaf we thought was a bird,
startle a woodcock from a tree. The warm air is an
embrace, we hope for a storm, feeling it near, the
migration of toads to our neighborhood pond.

The ones who come early chant for the others.
I hear their singing as a call to prayer.

Late Anniversary

No one told me that joy could be
as quiet as rain, that a clearing beyond
the flowering trees could hold us

To wander the woods with you
in muddy boots, to hear
the moaning of trees, to mourn their winter

To moulder and cackle, to leaf and split
to open to praise every green desire
to push through dirt and turn

To weather and womb, to praise and hunger
To lay full the table and fill the house
with people we love

To make green an offering
to wake, to bring
the thin flame of these hours

Before Bees

In rapture, this darling
whose lips elude force of God

To open slightly expose the tongue
to guilt, the force of guilt

Her body's marrow
The flower's bell shook awake

Fruit that never falls
Sweet air, before bees, before stinging

Even plants, the way they cradle rain,
I too feel my blood pull

Whose Woods

The noise of the bee was delight
Before Burning Forest Lane. Before
Wild Ginger Court. The meadow before
the complex. Humming its wheels or
mowing its Sunday. What passes
for religion. Before trillium and despair.

Narcissists preening the hedgerow

An exhibition of windows

His house is in the village though

God's Luck

When that great philanthropist aimed his cue ball
at the fallopian tube's center pocket
exothermic reaction, what some call the big bang
burned the world's whistling tea pot
to molten lava

Which is to say, he got lucky
and started a chain reaction
leading right up to now
a moment so big it keeps expanding
even as it collapses

Salt for Honey

Nettles: bring me a thunderstorm
Tempers collide above the steaming pot
Spinach hums in the background

Leeks chant: you've reached
the bottom of the pan
drink me slowly, like you mean it

Salt cries for honey, honey for salt
air doesn't move
potatoes boiling in a pan

Pesto nostalgic: where is my dill?
The chickpeas, lord, the chickpeas

Rain breaks and dill at last
speaks with authority

Grandmother's house
& summer's
a kettle boiling over

The Organizer

Her eyes hold a blue lark a wild streak
of what if, song
of you can't hold me back

The weather is changing, for months it's rained
when it should have been snow

That tattered sound of rain
stringing itself along, chill in the air
begging for bones

Where does the longevity of her idealism
come from, her flowering tenacity?

Think of the rain and how it won't stop
Believe in progress at a time when
everything is moving backward

Hold the course, whatever it is
hold the wheel, hold the phone

The wind is picking up, bringing
Seattle to New York. Crashing coastal
seizures into midwest bowling alleys
ripping out southern bayous

She carries on, says how can we stop?
We do what we do

Her eyes hold a blue lark
and behind her hundreds of people
with ribbons streaming on the wind.

University Kiss in a Time of War

Two slight young women—
the smaller one reaches for hands
leans close to give a kiss to the taller girl
an in between things kiss
a so long for now kiss
and nothing breaks, no alarms are sounded
no one is injured
Other students pass without
comment or craning
But the giver of the kiss looks back
a quick glance over her shoulder as if she's learned
that kisses can be dangerous
I'm reminded of children who live
on the border between wars
how farmers pay them
to go to rocky fields and find
landmines, small hands
mostly agile enough to keep the bombs
from exploding; the farmers
hungry to return to their fields

Lesson in Cuban Cooking

Wash the chicken in lime
Lift the embargo
Crush the ice and mint

Unify the ingredients
Evenly distribute
the pimentos

Let one side speak
to the other
until both are lucid

The rice steaming
on the table

Pete Tells Me Things

The tomato tree in his front yard for example
and the pond we'll dig at the top of the hill
despite the lack of water

The sunset breaks in office tower windows
and we're drinking red wine
from plastic hospital cups

When he coughs the stitches
in his chest pull loose
He tells me there was a shark
once in Micronesia

He slit its belly and watched it swim away
without a heart

When the Giraffes Come

The last days of July we walk past an oak struck by lightning
bark blown hundreds of feet above
the creek and hanging rocks
and Pete asks *will you put all of this in a poem?*
And will I include the part about giraffes
taking over the continent? And the elephants fucking
like it's a community event?

At breakfast beneath the dazzle of locust shells tied by string
above
the kitchen table he says

when the giraffes come we'll sneak to the fields
and cut the wire
so they can come and go as they please

Notes on the Poems

"Ghost Fishing Louisiana" for Damu Smith (1951-2006), environmental justice advocate.

'Einstein's Hands" inspired by Karsh photos.

"Pete Tells Me Things" and "When the Giraffes Come" for Pete Hill

"Time's Arrow" Inspired by Sugimoto's 2006 exhibit "History of History" at Freer Museum, in Washington, DC.

"Late Anniversary" for David R. Phillips.

"The Organizer" for Liz Walker and others who carry on.

"Monument" On March 23, 2003 a tobacco farmer and veteran from North Carolina drove his tractor into a pond near the Vietnam Memorial.

Gratitude

Much gratitude to the Provincetown Fine Arts Work Center, Ohio Arts Council, DC Commission on Arts and Humanities, and Blue Mountain Center for their generous support of this project.

A community of writers has nurtured these poems and my life as a writer. I am tremendously grateful to teachers and mentors, Jennifer Atkinson, Erin Belieu, Carolyn Forche, Eric Pankey, James Baker Hall, and Susan Tichy. I have learned so much from each of you.

Appreciation also to friends who read this manuscript or an earlier version, Michael J. Martinez for being one of my best readers, Jaime Lee Jarvis, who attended to details, Martha Collins for her intuitive sense of my work, careful reading and encouragement. Thank you also to E. Ethelbert Miller, who has taught me that being a writer is more than the words on the page. Thanks also to Sarah Browning and Christi Kramer, my cohorts in poetry in a time of war.

I also want to thank others who encouraged and commented on many of these poems or read the manuscript, Lauren Allyene, George Barnett, Paulette Beete, Brian Brodeur, Kiley Cogis Brodeur, Regie Cabico, Ashley Capps, Terri Cross Davis, Hayes Davis, Yael Flusberg, Joe Gouveia, Eleanor Graves, Christie Green, Sam Hammil, Fred Joiner, Joseph Ross, Tracy Knapp, Peter Montgomery, Nancy Pearson, Katy Richey, Jennifer Rouse, Susan Shied, Patricia Smith, Dan Vera, Pam Ushuck, and others. Deep appreciation also for my fellow fellows in Provincetown, Margaret Reges, Sara Eliza Johnson, Michael Morse, and Rebecca Lindenberg.

Thank you also to friends and family who have helped sustain me in this work and life, most especially my husband, David R. Phillips.

Enormous gratitude to John McKerman for your vision and work creating ABZ Press and enormous thanks to Charles Simic for selecting this book. It is a joy to have a poet I so admire choose my work.

Acknowledgments

Grateful Acknowledgement to the following publications where earlier versions of some of the poems in this book first appeared sometimes with different titles.

Beloit Poetry Journal: "Doing Hegel's Laundry" and "Silent Night"

Beltway Poetry Quarterly: "Time's Arrow"

Cincinnati Poetry Review: "Ghost Fishing Louisiana"

Day Eight: "Re: Salvadorian Generals"

Eleven, Eleven: "Rock Creek Park Runner"

Foreign Policy in Focus: "Full Snow Moon"

Gargoyle: "A Lesson in Cuban Cooking"

Hayden's Ferry Review: "Without a Map" and "Refrain"

Painted Bride Quarterly: "Portrait of my Father"

Phoebe: "Empty House," "Gauley River," and "When the Giraffes Come"

Poet Lore: "Aubade"

Poetry International: "Pete Tells Me Things"

Split This Rock Blog: "University Kiss in a Time of War"

Southeast Review: "Young Valley Farmers"

Terrain: "Last Time We Took A Family Vacation," "O, Piano" and "Whose Woods These Are"

Thanal Online: "National Zoo"

Witness: "The Wheel"

Poems have been included in or are forthcoming in the following anthologies: *Ecopoetry Anthology, Fire and Ink: An Anthology of Social Action Writing, Poets for Palestine Anthology, and Days I Moved Through Ordinary Sounds: The Teachers of Writers Corps in Poetry and Prose.*

A few early poems in this collection were published in *Rope as Witness* (Pudding House Press, 2007).

About the Author

Melissa Tuckey is poet, literary activist, and teacher who currently lives in Ithaca, New York. She is author of *Rope as Witness*, a chapbook published by Pudding House Press (2007). Her honors include a winter fellowship from the Provincetown Fine Arts Work Center, a residency at Blue Mountain Center, and individual artist awards DC Commission on the Arts and Humanities and Ohio Arts Council. Tuckey's poems have appeared widely in literary journals, including *Beloit Poetry Journal, Hayden's Ferry Review, Poet Lore, Witness,* and *Verse Daily,* and others. She holds an MA in literature from Ohio University and an MFA in poetry from George Mason University. Melissa Tuckey has a background in environmental activism and is a co-founder of Split This Rock, a national organization that celebrates poetry of witness and provocation.

CPSIA information can be obtained at www.ICGtesting.com
Printed in the USA
BVOW042041130213

313210BV00002B/17/P